MARTIAL ARTS

Ninjutsu

'Highly recommended reading for
any aspiring martial artist.
This series will enhance your
knowledge of styles, history,
grading systems and finding and
analyzing the right club.'

*Stan 'The Man' Longinidis
8-times World Kickboxing
Champion*

PAUL COLLINS

This edition first published in 2002 in the United States of America by
Chelsea House Publishers, a subsidiary of Haights Cross Communications.

Chelsea House Publishers
1974 Sproul Road, Suite 400
Broomall, PA 19008-0914

The Chelsea House world wide web address is www.chelseahouse.com

Library of Congress Cataloging-in-Publication Data Applied for.

ISBN 0-7910-6871-4

First published in 2002 by
MACMILLAN EDUCATION AUSTRALIA PTY LTD
627 Chapel Street, South Yarra, Australia 3141

Copyright © Paul Collins 2002

Text design by Judith Summerfeldt Grace and Karen Nettelfield
Cover design by Judith Summerfeldt Grace
Edited by Carmel Heron

Printed in China

Acknowledgments
Photographs by Nick Sandalis, except p. 9 © Geostock,
pp. 25 and 27 courtesy of Mark Lutman.

The author would like to thank: Daniel Curmi, Sempai, from the Kevin
Hawthorne Ninja Schools, PO Box 316, Kilsythe, Vic 3137, Australia; Mark
Lutman, The Shinobi-Kai Ninpo Bugei Ryu Ha, PO Box 6386, Basingstoke
Hampshire, RG24 9YG, United Kingdom, www.shinobi-kai.com; Jim
Gould (NZ) www.yamajutsu-kai.com

**Techniques used in this book should only be practiced under qualified
supervision.**

Contents

What are martial arts?

Most people have seen at least one fantastic martial arts movie. A lot of it is trick photography. A **ninja** cannot really jump backwards and land on the roof of a towering house! Then again, martial arts are about belief—belief in yourself and your ability to overcome any obstacle, no matter how big or small.

Ask any martial arts student why they train and the answer will be to learn **self-defense**. But that answer only scratches the surface of the term 'martial arts'.

One of the many functions of martial arts is to train students, both physically and mentally.

Martial arts have ancient traditions steeped in discipline and dedication. Most martial arts have developed from ancient Asian combat skills. In **feudal** times, people in Asia had to defend themselves against attack. Quite often, peasants were not allowed to carry weapons, so self-defense became their weapon.

Some martial arts are fighting sports, such as karate and kung fu. Other martial arts, like tai chi, concentrate on self-improvement, although self-defense is part of the training.

Kendo

Muay Thai

Karate

Dedication and discipline

Ninjutsu is hard work. Ask any senior student. Dedication plays a major role in the life of a martial arts student. Training can be up to four times a week, and an average session lasts about two hours.

Students practice one simple procedure over and over again. They might repeat a simple move 200 times in one training session, only to repeat the same move the next time they train. Martial artists learn through repetition, so that even the most basic techniques can be automatically performed when they are suddenly required.

The word 'martial' comes from Mars, the Roman god of war.

It's a fact!

Ninjutsu

Understanding ninjutsu

Ninjutsu is considered one of the 'heavier' martial arts, as opposed to the 'softer' martial arts such as taekwondo and judo.

Ninjutsu is a martial art that involves striking with the feet, hands, knees, elbows—in fact, every part of you is a weapon. A ninjutsu student, known as a ninja, concentrates on putting as much power as possible into the point of impact of a strike.

The hands, balls of the feet, heels, forearms, knees and elbows are used to strike an opponent. Padded surfaces or wood are used to toughen up these areas during practice. However, timing, tactics and mental attitude are all considered just as important to a ninja as physical toughness.

Weapon training plays a large part in ninjutsu. The same amount of training is devoted to defending against weapon attacks as is devoted to teaching **offensive** tactics. For instance, ninja learn how to avoid a staff attack. These days it is unlikely that an opponent would be holding a staff in a real-life situation, but this teaches students how to avoid an opponent armed with a long pole, for example.

A double side kick is practiced against two attackers.

Ninjutsu is not as popular as karate or taekwondo, so good clubs are hard to find. Each club has its own training methods, and some use techniques from other martial arts. However, all ninjutsu clubs teach the importance of respect for fellow students and instructors, and the importance of good mental attitude.

Other benefits of learning ninjutsu include:

◉ general fitness

◉ inner peace and calm

◉ self-control and well being

◉ precision and speed

◉ self-discipline and confidence

◉ making friends.

These days, authentic ninjutsu is not taught in most schools. The original ninja were masters at horse riding, archery, sword fighting, **espionage** and **assassination.** Most ninja were born into ninja families and trained their whole lives. They became experts at mixing poisons, cooking, survival in the wild, swimming and many different combat skills. All of this cannot be taught in a *dojo* part-time!

Japan: the birthplace of ninjutsu

Population:	126.2 million
Language:	Japanese
Currency:	Yen (¥)
Main religions:	Shinto, Buddhism and Christianity

Japan leads the world as a fishing nation. This is because it is a nation of mountainous islands in the North Pacific Ocean. The four main islands are Honshu, Kyushu, Shikoku and Hokkaido. They are situated off the mainland of east Asia. Tokyo, on the island of Honshu, is the capital city of Japan.

Many of Japan's mountains are active volcanoes, which often cause earthquakes. Mount Fuji is Japan's tallest mountain. It is 3,776 meters (12,390 feet) high and it is an extinct volcano.

The government of Japan is a democratic government, elected by the people. The head of government is the Prime Minister. The Emperor of Japan is the ceremonial head of state.

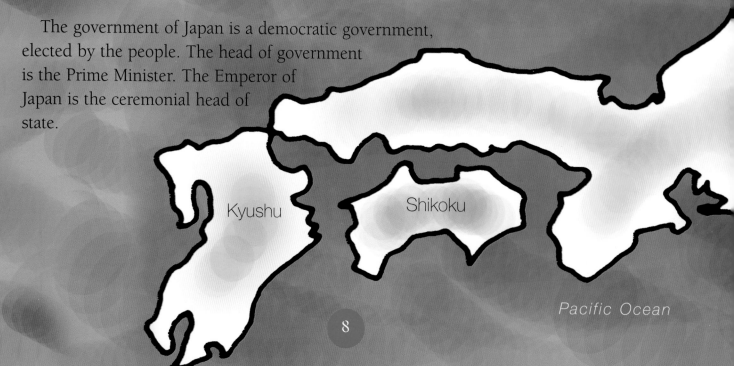

Kyushu

Shikoku

Pacific Ocean

Hokkaido

Miyajima Island, Japan

Sea of Japan

Honshu

Pacific Ocean

Mount Fuji ▲   ■ Tokyo

Ninjutsu was only practiced in a small area of Japan: the Iga and Koga mountains on the island of Honshu.

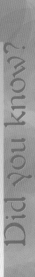

Did you know?

The history of ninjutsu

Because of the secrecy surrounding ninja, little is known of their full history. The traditions of the ninja are more than 1,100 years old. The mountain-dwelling families of central Honshu, the largest of the Japanese islands, developed ninjutsu.

It is believed that the methods used in ninjutsu came from China. When the T'ang dynasty fell, a great many **philosophers**, warriors and other people fled the new Chinese rulers and escaped to Japan. Ninja families became exposed to new ideas and these formed the basis of the martial art that became known as ninjutsu.

Only people born into ninja families practiced ninjutsu. The ninja families were not warlike. They were heavily taxed and looked down on by the ruling society because they were considered outsiders who kept to themselves. The ninja clans soon became experts at gathering political information. They were vastly outnumbered by the **samurai** clans, so the ninja used **guerrilla warfare** tactics and more devious means to play the warlike samurai clans against one another and to distract them.

'Ninjutsu' translated means 'art of **stealth**' or 'the techniques of stealing in'. The ninja devised special ways of walking and running, which disguised the direction they were travelling in, to confuse anyone following them.

Some ninja hired themselves out as assassins and **saboteurs**. They used their training to **infiltrate** enemy lines and kill important people. Among other things, ninja were masters of disguise. They were often confused with the yamabushi (wandering priests) because they sometimes dressed up like them to enter enemy territory.

Defense against two opponents

Because ninja belonged to a secret society, many myths started about them. They were often thought of as magicians or wizards because of their seeming ability to disappear. They were, however, simply masters of using shadows and any obstacles to hide themselves. Moonlight often provided ninja with shadows in which to 'disappear'.

After completing missions ninja would flee using props to help them. Pursuers, who usually only wore straw sandals, could easily step on sharp metal spikes (called *tetsu-bishi*, or caltrops) that the ninja would sprinkle on the ground behind them. Other items in their bag of nasty tricks included blinding pepper powder, blow guns, poisons and *kuda-yari*, short telescopic spears that suddenly became very long spears. All of these items helped make ninja the infamous figures they are known as today.

The Japanese government became so fearful of the ninja that in the 1600s the study of ninjutsu was banned. To even mention the name was a crime punishable by death. Ninjutsu in a different form has now been revived due to the fairly recent popularity of the martial arts.

Dress code and etiquette

Dress code

The ninjutsu uniform, called a *gi*, is usually black. Like most other martial arts uniforms, the *gi* looks like a pair of loose-fitting pajamas with a belt around the waist. The uniform is lightweight and comfortable. There are no zippers, buttons or pockets that might cause injury to others while training.

The parts of the ninjutsu uniform are:

◉ *dogi*, the pants and jacket

◉ *obi*, the belt

◉ *tabi*, the split-toe shoe.

The *obi* can be any color. The *tabi* have rubber soles to aid stealth.

Traditionally, ninja hid their identities with the utmost care and wearing a mask was essential.

How to tie a ninja's mask

1 The hood is tied at the back of the head.

2 The second piece is tied next.

3 The mask is sometimes joined together like a **balaclava**.

Etiquette

Ninjutsu schools require students to show proper respect for their **sensei**, fellow students and *dojo*.

- Bow when entering or leaving a *dojo*. Bowing at the start and end of practice is considered a sign of respect for your opponent.

- Do not stand with your back to the **joseki**, train in front of the *joseki* or walk directly in front of the *joseki*.

- Never walk directly across the *dojo*, always walk around the outside of the training area.

- Never walk in front of anyone without indicating your wish to do so and being given permission to do so.

- Jewelry, such as earrings and necklaces, is not worn while training. Any jewelry that cannot be removed must be taped over as it can cause injury if it becomes snagged.

- Swearing will not be tolerated in the *dojo*.

- Outdoor shoes are not to be worn in the *dojo*. Barefoot or *tabi* are the only acceptable footwear.

- Never sit with the soles of the feet facing the instructor or other students.

- Ninjutsu techniques are not to be demonstrated outside of the *dojo*.

- Outside of the *dojo*, techniques must only be used for self-defense and then only as a last resort. The techniques learned in ninjutsu should never be abused.

- Eating, drinking (except water) and smoking are not permitted in the *dojo*.

- A high standard of personal hygiene is required. Clean *gi* should be worn at all times. Fingernails and toenails must be clipped short. Long hair must be tied and not hang loose.

Bowing is considered a sign of respect

Before you start

Choosing a club

A look through the telephone book under the general heading 'Martial Arts' will show you where the nearest clubs are.

It is better to join a large club with many members. Find out if the club has students about your own age. If not, you could always join with a friend. Unlike most other martial arts schools, ninjutsu schools do not actively seek younger members. It is a good idea to telephone a club and speak to an instructor first.

If money is a consideration, phone around and compare costs. Some clubs charge a joining fee, while other clubs only charge per visit. Visitors normally do not pay, so it is a good idea to sit in on a session or two before joining a club.

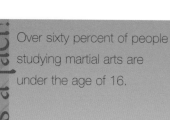

It's a fact!
Over sixty percent of people studying martial arts are under the age of 16.

Students from a ninjutsu club

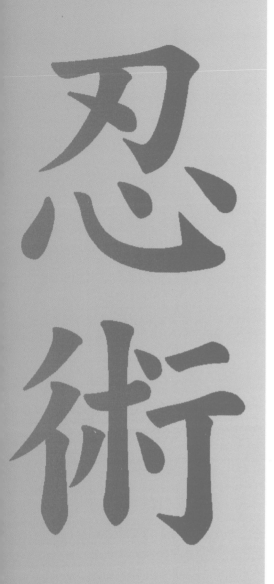

Clothing and equipment

It is not expensive to start ninjutsu. Your first few training sessions can be performed in a pair of loose pants and a T-shirt.

Clubs should have all the protective equipment you will need, like leg and arm guards, although it is better to buy your own once you start to train seriously. Personal equipment can be kept in better condition and will fit better than the standard club equipment. Second-hand padded guards and even gloves can be bought at recycled equipment stores and through personal advertisements in newspapers. Garage sales are also a good source of second-hand martial arts equipment.

Many clubs have their own stores where students can purchase equipment at discount prices. Other clubs have private deals with specialty stores and members can produce their club cards to obtain discounts.

Club badges are usually bought directly from the club. Most clubs insist that students sew them onto uniforms before training.

Insurance

Insurance is advised, although you are unlikely to get badly injured at a well-run martial arts club. Most clubs have insurance coverage so it pays to ask.

Confidence and disabilities

Everyone feels nervous when they first enter a club. Once you have met some fellow students you will feel a lot more confident.

A light stretching workout just before competition is a good way to relax and to loosen stiff muscles. Good instructors will teach you breathing techniques, which will calm you and help you to focus.

A disability should not stop you from trying ninjutsu. Many top athletes have **asthma**. Other athletes have **diabetes**. Getting fit through ninjutsu can help improve your overall condition. Just make sure your instructor knows of your complaint, take necessary precautions and bow out when you do not feel well.

Man cannot discover new oceans until he has the courage to lose sight of the shore.

Anonymous

Fitness and training

Beginner martial artists are not usually ready for serious training. This takes time. They need to build fitness slowly. Most martial arts clubs have beginners' classes, where students learn the basic techniques and get fit.

At the start of each training session, students perform warm-up and stretching exercises. The instructor will then teach the class something new or ask students to practice a certain technique with a partner. Partner training teaches timing, reaction, balance, self-control and counter attack skills.

Fitness is important for all martial arts.

A training session can last anywhere from 90 minutes to two hours. A typical session includes:

- **meditation** (to release tension and become focused)

- stretching (to gain mobility and flexibility)

- contact training (to toughen your body against attack)

- self-defense (learning how to defend yourself on the street)

- weapon training (mastering weapons such as the sword and **shuriken**)

- perception and sensory training (learning to be alert to all attacks)

- philosophy (to help self-awareness).

18

Stretching

As well as fitness you will need to gain flexibility and greater mobility. This means stretching all your body parts. You need to loosen and warm tight and cold muscles.

It is important to keep each stretching movement gentle and slow. You should not use jerking or bouncing movements.

Stretching has many purposes. It:

- increases heart and lung capacity
- helps you practice movements you are about to perform
- helps avoid injury from pulled muscles
- gives you greater flexibility.

It is equally important to cool down after exercising. This maintains the level of blood circulation and reduces muscle spasms. Gentle cool-down stretches also help prevent injuries, because they reduce muscle tightness.

Hamstring stretch

Hamstring stretch

Groin stretch

Hamstring and back stretch

Sparring

Sparring is when you practice what you have learned with a partner. Most sparring is performed using full contact, so students must learn how to take a hit as well as how to deliver one. Students can develop their techniques against opponents to see what works for them and what does not. When sparring, a student does not know which techniques their partner is going to use, and timing and precision become very important.

Sparring is not competitive as there is no winner or loser. It is a method of practicing so that students learn from one another.

There are few competitions in ninjutsu. Some clubs may hold archery or *shuriken-*throwing competitions, but it is not common practice.

Students spar against more than one opponent.

Games

Contests and games are sometimes part of a training session, and some instructors pick teams to compete against one another.

One game involves throwing a *shuriken* at a partner. If you are hit, you have to do push-ups. In a team contest version of the game, two sides throw rubber *shuriken* at a target about 3–4.5 meters (10–15 feet) away. The team that loses has to do push-ups.

The idea of these games is to have fun but at the same time learn hand–eye coordination. A variation to the game is if you are hit in the arm, you 'lose' that arm, or if hit in the leg, you 'lose' that leg, and so on. So if you are hit in the leg, you have to hop. If you are hit in your throwing arm, then you have to throw with your other arm.

A rubber shuriken

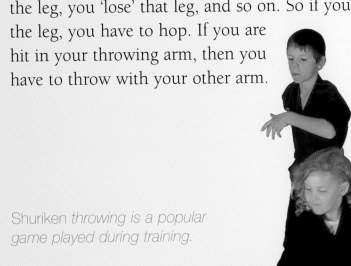

Shuriken *throwing is a popular game played during training.*

21

Ninjutsu techniques

Ninjutsu schools teach both unarmed self-defense techniques and weapon training. Where most martial arts specialize in grappling and throwing, or kicking and punching, or even just weapons, ninjutsu teaches students all the aspects of every technique.

You will find some moves easier to master than others. But you should practice all techniques, even those that you do not like. It is also important to learn all techniques with both left and right hands and feet. It is equally important to learn how to defend yourself against various kicks and punches to both sides of your body.

The same applies to throws and being thrown. Students learn how to throw opponents over both shoulders, and how to land safely after being thrown over both the right and left shoulder.

Weapon training is also taught so students are capable of handling all sorts of weapons with both hands. Originally this was so that if a ninja was injured, they could still fight using their other hand or leg.

1 *The student facing gets a firm grip of his opponent.*

2 *The same student twists and thrusts his hip into his opponent's hip with slightly bent legs.*

22

Throws

There are countless throwing techniques in martial arts. These are usually done by unbalancing an opponent and applying leverage or force to throw them. Rather than pull back when an opponent grabs you, the idea is to give into that pull and not resist it. By doing this, you can unbalance your opponent because they expect you to pull back.

③ *The student then thrusts up, pulling his opponent up and to the side.*

④ *The student restrains his opponent and is now ready to finish the fight.*

Kicks

Because legs are longer than arms, they are effective with distance strikes. For example, a kick can reach further than a punch. Legs also have the advantage over punching because a kick is delivered with assistance from the hips, which gives it greater power.

A kick can reach further than a punch.

Punches

Beginners learn simple punching techniques. Always strike with the first two knuckles, because these are the biggest and strongest. Never bend your wrist when you strike. Keep the wrist in a straight line with your forearm.

Practicing a punch

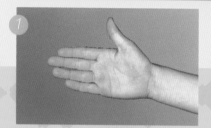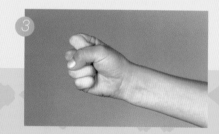

How to form a fist

1
2
3

Holds

Once you have your opponent on the mat, you apply pressure. Your opponent should tap either you or the mat in submission if they are unable to break the hold. Armlocks are carried out by applying leverage to an opponent's arm to restrain them. Strangleholds are when an opponent is restrained from behind and gripped around the neck and upper body.

An armlock

Combination techniques

Single techniques do not always work, especially if your opponent is as experienced as you are. Therefore a series of moves may be essential. These are called combination techniques.

For example, if you successfully block an opponent's punch, your opponent might then counter defend by clasping your wrist. You then need to break from the wristlock and perform another technique.

Upper block

Lower block against kick

Kata

Kata are a series of movements, known as forms or patterns. They are designed for students to practice skills that have been learned. There are many *kata* in ninjutsu. The first set of five basic techniques are called *sanshin no kata* (three hearts techniques). These techniques are taught so that students become familiar with distance, proper timing and position. These are all important in studying ninjutsu.

The *kihon happo* contains a set of eight techniques that teach arm locks, throws and strikes. Most of the ninjutsu techniques are based on this set of patterns.

Kamae no kata: *this is one of the first kata that students learn. It teaches students the basic moves that they will learn as ninja.*

25

Ninjutsu weapons

The history of weaponry dates back to feudal times. Peasants were not allowed to carry weapons so they developed skills with everyday objects. The pole, or staff, became a lethal weapon. Since ninja often posed as monks to disguise themselves, they would carry a long pole to help walk the long miles between villages. The ninja, like the peasants, knew how to use a pole as a weapon. A shorter pole could look like a walking stick, yet kill an enemy if used with skill. A longer pole could easily unseat horsemen, or topple a galloping horse if placed within its legs.

Today, students usually learn the basics of ninjutsu without the weapons. More emphasis is placed on defense against weapons than the use of them. For instance, students learn to duck, jump and roll away from a staff attack. The staff or pole is usually about 1–2 meters (3–6 feet) long and made from rubber. Students also learn how to avoid *shuriken*. Although these are made from rubber for training purposes, students sometimes wear protective eyeglasses in case of injury.

All weapon training is introduced to students after they have been training for several years, or when the head instructor feels that the student is ready. There is no minimum age at which students can be introduced to weapons as long as they are made fully aware of all the safety aspects when using them.

Students practicing swordfighting with a shinai (bamboo stick)

The ninjas' **arsenal** contained swords, spears, **staves** and other equipment. The ninjas' favorite weapon was the *kyotetsu-koge*, a two-bladed dagger. One blade was curved, and the other straight. These were sometimes joined to a rope by a metal ring and could be hurled and retrieved—a bit like a sharp-bladed **boomerang**! Ninja were also extremely accurate with a blowgun that fired poisoned darts.

Another of their weapons was the *shuriken*. This was a small iron shape that had six to eight sharp poisoned tips. The *shuriken* was placed between thumb and forefinger and it could be thrown with great accuracy. *Shuriken* could be disguised as medallions around the neck on a chain. A quick tug and a *shuriken* could be thrown at an attacker with power and accuracy. Although not lethal, the *shuriken* slowed down any attackers.

Ninja scaled walls by using a *shuko*, which was an iron gauntlet studded with sharp points. This could also be used as a lethal weapon against an attacker. *Shuko* were usually worn with hooked sandals that assisted in keeping a firm grip when scaling.

A ninja's arsenal: (from top to bottom) bo (six-foot staff), jo (four-foot staff), hanbo (three-foot staff), ninja to, bokken (wooden sword), kusari tundo (weighted chain) and kyotetsu-koge; (bottom row, from left to right) shuko, shuriken (throwing blade) and tessen (war fan).

The *tanto* knife was the favored weapon of the ninja, simply because it was small and easily hidden. The ninja's sword was also shorter than the samurai sword, because the ninja usually attacked with speed, and then disappeared into the night. A longer sword would have slowed them down, and it was not usually the ninja's way to fight on a battlefield.

An innocent-looking fan was also a dangerous weapon in the hands of a ninja. The *tessen* was steel-edged and could slice through an enemy as easily as a razor blade.

27

The language of ninjutsu

Most commands you hear in ninjutsu are spoken in Japanese. It is a sign of respect to know Japanese. A ninjutsu student can travel anywhere in the world and understand the language of ninjutsu.

Japanese words sound the way they are written. For instance, *sensei* is pronounced 'sen-say'. 'G' is pronounced like the 'g' in 'get', not like the 'g' in 'gentle'. 'I' is pronounced 'ee'.

To learn ninjutsu, you will need to know some of the following expressions. Some of the terms can vary from club to club.

chudan	'ready' position
dojo	training hall
hajime	start
kamae	stance or position
kata	preset patterns to train students
keiko	free practice, sparring without set patterns
kiai	made up from *ki,* meaning 'spirit', and *ai,* meaning 'meeting'. A shout to produce more power and energy when striking
mate	wait
mokuso	meditation
rei	a bow
ryu	schools

sensei	instructor	
shihan	senior teacher	
soke	Grandmaster, a top-ranking teacher	
tobi	jumping techniques	
yame	stop	
yoko aruki	sideways walking	

Did you know?

In Japanese, the singular and plural forms of a word are often the same. For instance, the plural of *dojo* is *dojo* and the plural of 'samurai' is still 'samurai'.

Counting one to ten

ichi	one	1
ni	two	2
san	three	3
shi	four	4
go	five	5
roku	six	6
shichi	seven	7
hachi	eight	8
ku	nine	9
ju	ten	10

Ninja sayings

All martial arts have a history. The masters who originally founded each martial art wrote down their techniques and thoughts so they would never be forgotten. These texts also included sayings about how ninjutsu students should live their lives.

The first rule of ninjutsu is don't get hit!
The second rule is don't forget the first rule.

You cannot cross a river in two jumps.

When you come to the mountain it is easier to walk around than to climb over but you will miss the view from the top!

We were all born originals—do not let us die copies.

To be upset over what you do not have is to waste what you do have.

The man who removes a mountain begins by carrying away small stones.

Often the impossible is what has not been attempted.

The wise man seeks solutions, the ignorant man only casts blame.

Happiness is a condition of the mind, not a result of circumstances.

Within every problem lies the seed of its solution.

Treat mistakes as lessons.

Patience in a moment of anger will save a hundred days of sorrow.

Glossary

arsenal	store of weapons
assassination	when someone is murdered by a hired killer
asthma	a breathing disorder
balaclava	a head piece to shield against the cold
boomerang	a curved stick, which returns in flight to the thrower
Buddhism	a religion that started in Asia
diabetes	a disease where the body does not fully process sugar
dojo	training hall
espionage	spying
feudal	dating back to the Middle Ages, when all the land was owned by the nobility and the peasants worked for them
guerrilla warfare	when small teams of soldiers hit and run
infiltrate	to get behind enemy lines without being detected
joseki	(also called the *kamiza*) an area of the *dojo* regarded as the 'high place'. It is generally on the north-facing wall of the *dojo* and is where the altar would be set up. It is also the side the masters and instructors sit or stand facing the class
meditation	deep and serious thinking
ninja	traditionally a spy or assassin
offensive	attacking rather than retreating
philosophers	people who have theories about the meanings of things
saboteurs	people who wreck plans or property
samurai	Japanese warriors of ancient Japan
self-defense	usually grappling, which involves pinning your opponent so that they cannot strike you
sensei	instructor
Shinto	Japanese religion that worships ancestors
shuriken	throwing blade
staves	long wooden poles
stealth	being quiet, secretive

Index